The Art of Creative Drawing

Animal Designs and Totems

Written and Illustrated by
Greg C Grace

This edition produced for
Eagle Editions Ltd.
11 Heathfield
Royston
Hertfordshire SG8 5BW

ISBN: 1 902328 48 5

**Eagle
Editions**

Printed in Malaysia

Overview of the Series

The Art of Creative Drawing series explores the world of symbolism and art with an emphasis on tapping into our deeper creative potential. Working through each book gives an opportunity to explore and develop drawing skills, while enhancing intuitive and previously untapped talents. Simple step-by-step explanations guide you on a journey of knowledge and creativity, catering for the budding, amateur and professional artist. As well as information and exercises you will find completed images available for colouring. The series is appropriate for young people, experimenting with and further exploring earlier teachings. Visual art students, either in high school or at university level, or for anyone captivated by colour, shapes, symbols and the combination within.

Workbook 1:

Universal and Multicultural Symbols: Enhancing Creativity and Intuition focuses on the design of mandalas as they have been used traditionally around the world. Exploring the meaning and relationship between shapes and symbols you will learn to create symbolic mandalas in a practical way, resulting in inspiring pieces of art.

Workbook 2:

Animal Symbolism, Totems and the Language of Shapes explores the dynamic energies of animal symbolism and totems in relation to mandalas. It focuses on associations between shapes and animals, allied with natural principles.

Workbook 3:

Colour Symbolism, Shapes and the Process of Creation shows the traditional symbolism of colour as used in creative artwork by various cultures. It explains how colour is used in design, highlighting many of nature's processes. The magnificent richness of colour plays a practical and symbolic role in explaining both meanings and visual effect.

Workbook 4:

The Geometry of Nature, Symbols and Archetypal Shapes details the use of geometry in drawing and design. Exploring basic geometric and archetypal shapes it shows how these are used as structural foundations for mandalas while creating balanced images. Geometric borders and designs are presented as accompaniments recognising the importance of balance and harmony.

With over 100 images and designs this series offers inspirational and user-friendly techniques when developing and guiding the practitioner toward accomplishing truly significant art pieces.

The Art Of Creative Drawing

Contents

Introduction

The series has several primary objectives which are intended to assist the practitioner in developing more creative thought and application. These unique elements and combinations, whilst unusual, have been developed from early cultures such as Tibetan, American Indian, Arabic, Mayan and Indian.

Working with animals and plant symbols, geometric shapes and structure, together with the nature of colour, these art works are refreshingly inspirational. The majority of these pieces are produced within mandalas. The mandala dates back centuries and is known to cover all continents.

The purpose of the mandala is to explain mythological stories and culturally distinctive artwork. Unlike western art, as we understand it, these pieces derive from the natural world and spiritual understanding.

Each element of a mandala has meaning and represents some guiding aspects or principle. Geometry and placement of animal symbols play a significant part in explaining quite intricate elements and colour is used to structurally enhance, not simply embellish.

This series will inevitably educate and enthrall all age groups ranging from early teenage through to advancing years.

Things You Will Need

To complete the exercises in this book you will need some simple drawing tools. Most of these are inexpensive, easy to obtain and include basic equipment such as pencils, eraser, transparent ruler, compass and paper. As you become confident with your drawing skills there is no end to the creative ways you can colour your designs and your local art supplier will be able to advise you on the available range of quality paper and colouring pencils, markers and paints.

Compass: for drawing circles and aligning curved shapes. Look for one which allows you to change the pencil and thereby incorporate coloured pencils and markers.

Eraser: a good quality soft white eraser is preferable as it will help keep clean paper .

Ruler: for drawing straight lines and making accurate measurements.
A transparent plastic ruler is most effective as it allows you to align your measurements with other shapes.

1 2 3 4 5 6 7 8 9 10 11 12 13 14 15 16 17 18 19 20 21 22 23 24 25 26 27 28 29 30

Paper: for practise and drawing your finished designs
clean white A4 size sheets of bond paper are ideal;
however for a better finish you may wish to use a quality art paper.

Pencils: for drawing your designs, including guidelines and outlines. Graphite pencils are preferred, particularly the HB grade as this is neither too dark nor light and can easily be erased. Coloured pencils are ideal for defining and colouring your finished designs. Harder art quality pencils are better for defining lines and edges while soft pencils are preferable for a smooth finish.

How to Use This Book

The Art of Creative Drawing series has been designed using both traditional freehand and geometric drawing methods. Innovative exercises are aimed at awakening your artistic potential through the creative use of lines, shapes, symbols and geometry. Although this is fundamentally a drawing book, colour has been added to highlight the symbolic qualities of different shapes and images.

General Drawing Tips

- For each exercise A4 size paper is recommended, though once feeling confident mandalas can be created to any size. Drawing at a larger scale simply requires extensions of established proportions.

- For each exercise we recommend drawing a square 180mm x180mm to act as an outer border. Exact measurements for creating each design are given. Where visual examples are enlarged (to highlight a step) or reduced (to see the bigger picture) simply follow the written instructions. Examples on page 13 show how shapes and sizes can be increased.

- When drawing new shapes and symbols you might like to practise on a separate sheet of paper until pleased with the result (this can save unnecessary pencil lines and erasing). Using a separate sheet also allows to trace your image a number of times until you are confident when drawing more spontaneously. This is particularly important where repetition and symmetry is needed.

- If you have trouble seeing through the paper when tracing images hold it to the light, against a window or active computer screen.

- Keep pencil guidelines clear, yet faint, as when these are finished with you will carefully erase. To highlight and colour your finished artwork you may use coloured pencils (for a soft look), art-quality pens or markers (for a more defined finish), gouache (for rich colour) or art-quality acrylic paint (ideal for larger designs), or any combination which suits. Experiment with each for different effects.

Drawing Circles and Squares

- Drawing circles and squares with a ruler or compass is the most accurate and precise method. However, most of the colouring designs were composed freehand.

Using What You Learn

- The information and exercises in this book lay the foundation for learning to draw mandalas. While there are guidelines to help you create symbolically rich designs there are no firm rules. There is no end to the wide range of designs you can create. Part of learning to draw is using your imagination and trusting yourself. More than anything the drawing experience should be enjoyable. Allow yourself to be open, and experiment.

Exercise 1: Animals and Nature

In this exercise we will create a mandala depicting the relationship between animals and the outer world. Based on a foundation of the four directions we will use nature's symbols and animal totems to portray some diverse characteristics, incorporating the elements (earth, air, fire and water). (To preview the finished image turn to page 11). East is positioned at the top as this is how it is traditionally represented in the mandala.

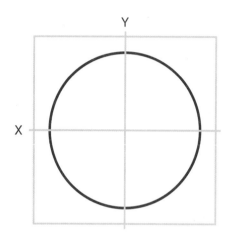

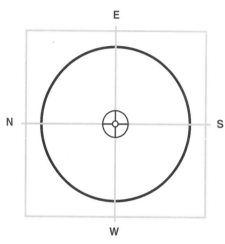

Step 1: Draw a 180mm square, faintly adding the midlines for the vertical (Y) and horizontal (X) axis to obtain the centre point. Placing your compass in the centre draw a large circle approximately 80% of the paper's width. The square acts as the earth and the circle our creative potential.

Step 2: Add a small circle in the centre, approximately 5% the width of the first circle. Add a second slightly larger circle approximately four times its size. Use the above image as a guide for ratios, however the exact size is not important. Connect the two inner circles along the faint horizontal and vertical lines as shown. This central image is a traditional symbol used by Native American Indians to represent Mother Earth and the four directions North, South, East and West.

Step 3: Draw two diagonal lines joining opposite corners of the square. Draw a third central circle (A) approximately twice the size of the second inner circle; this will provide a base on which to draw the mountains and a space in which to later add elements. Draw a mountain on the upper vertical line as shown with its tip approximately two-thirds the distance to the outer circle and its base almost touching the diagonal guides. You can copy this image or create your own. The mountain represents the mineral kingdom and our connection to the earth.

Hints

Draw all lines and images faintly in pencil until you are happy with the final design.

Erase all guidelines before adding colour with pencils, inks or paints.

At this stage keep images simple and be spontaneous in your drawing.

Step 4: The remaining mountains need to be added for the other directions. To make them the same height use the compass to measure the tip distance and mark this on the remaining three lines. While the proportions should be close it is not crucial they all be identical. Next draw a tree on the upper left diagonal line; for example, a pine tree as shown this upper image or an ever-green tree as shown below. Feel free to choose a type of tree to represent the nature of the mandala you wish to produce. These should be approximately the same height as the mountains.

Step 5: Add the remaining three trees on the diagonal guidelines between the mountains to seal in the less stable energies of the corner directions. These represent the vegetable kingdom.

Symbolism

The tree represents earth meeting heaven (striving upwards to the vastness of the sky) and also heaven meeting earth (reaching down through the earth's interior). It also explains protection and groundedness, representing the resources provided by nature in fruits, nuts, seeds, woods and oils.

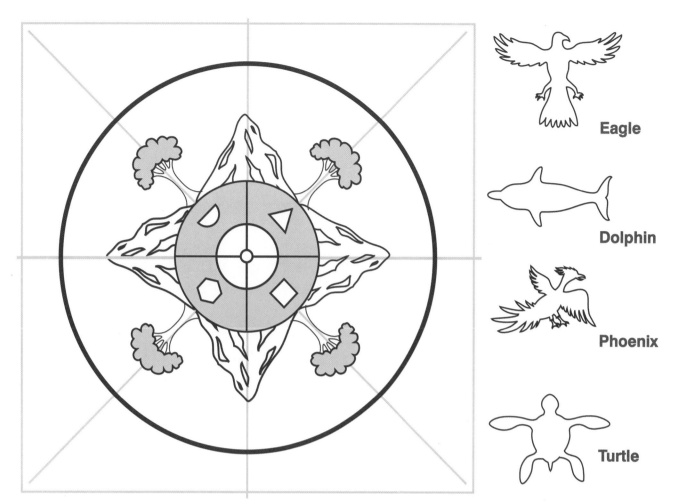

Eagle

Dolphin

Phoenix

Turtle

Step 6: Add symbols representing the elements. With the four geometric shapes in the larger central circle representing these elements water, fire, earth and air, from the top left segment around in a clockwise direction. Position these on the diagonal guidelines in the centre of the circle.

Step 7: Finally, draw the four animal totems as shown in the final image. Their qualities relate to each of four the elements and directions. You might like to practise by first copying or tracing these on a separate sheet of paper, then adding to your design. Their tips should be just inside the outer circle and their base resting on the mountain top. For hints in colouring your finished art, refer to the animal and colour symbolism sections at the end of the book.

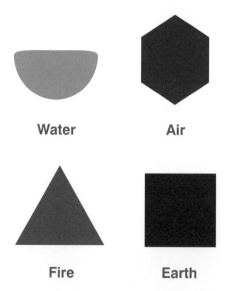

Water   **Air**

Fire   **Earth**

Observations

Drawing animal totems in mandalas is best done in simple outline form as only symbolism is required. It is also an easier way to practice your drawing skills, although as confidence grows you can be more expressive. Traditional cultures use natures symbols and animal totems in sacred ways adding depth and meaning to artistic imagery.

This mandala uses a diverse range of simple, yet meaningful, symbols. The square represents the earth as a foundation while the outer circle the cosmos and our potential, as well as principles of unity and equality. The central circle relates to the elements and four directions of Mother Earth, and the middle circle, the mountains meeting our journey. The mountains are our connection to the earth, and trees, the joining of heaven and earth. The animal totems depict the four directions in many cultures and each represents different qualities. Vision, wisdom and air (the eagle), freedom, playfulness, communication and water (the dolphin), passivity, groundedness and earth (the turtle) and victory, personal achievement and the transforming qualities of fire (the phoenix). This artwork is featured in colour on the front cover.

Animal Symbolism and Shapes

The symbolism of nature can be seen in basic geometric shapes, such as a pentagonal five-petalled flower or hexagonal snow-flake crystal and in the symmetrical outline of forms, such as a bird in flight. Here are examples of geometric symbolism in animals (including birds, mammals and insects). Viewing animals in symbolic ways helps create more meaningful images and designs, blending animal totems with structure and artistic expression.

Butterfly

The butterfly represents a four-point square, as well as the ellipse shape reflected in its body and wings. The more dynamic shape of the diamond is shown in its chrysalis form promoting new life as it emerges from the cocoon. Yellow tones of spring and violet tones are associated with transformation.

Dolphin

A basic five-point geometry of the pentagon can be shown in the dolphin (as well as the whale and human being). Dolphins portray dynamic and playful energies, self-expression and communication and are associated with the green and aqua tones.

Bird

Many birds can represent the six-point geometry of the hexagon. Reptiles, such as the lizard, also relate to six-point geometry, however these resonate with different colours depending on their stage of evolution. Birds can be coloured with green, aqua blue and violet tones depending on the energy being depicted. Doves can be coloured white or soft blue to reflect purity and peace, while the eagle is associated with violet tones for transcendence.

Spider

The spider is one of the more obvious creatures relating to eight-point octagonal geometry. Through its web of life it has a deeper association with structure and the infinite possibilities of creation. it relates well to indigo and blue tones. Its eight legs promote the four winds of change and four directions on the Native American Indian medicine wheel.

Archetypal Shapes

When the geometric shapes (triangle, square, pentagon etc.) are placed within a circle they provide an ideal foundation on which to design a mandala. Use any one of the archetypal shapes below when you want to construct a balanced and symmetrical mandala.

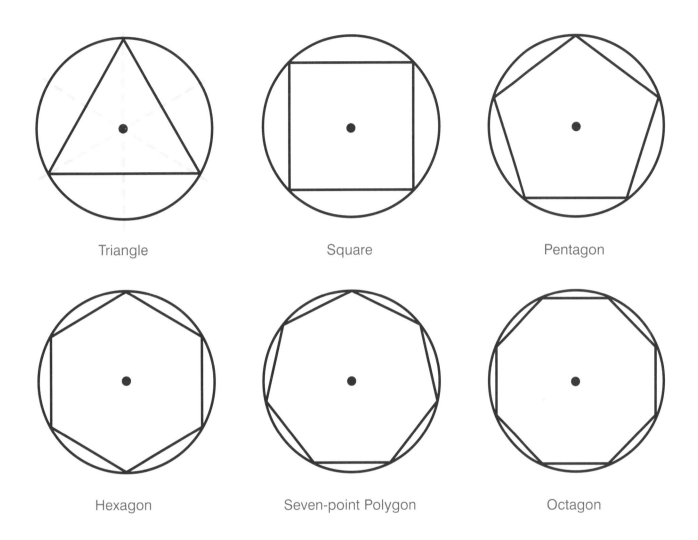

Triangle	Square	Pentagon
Hexagon	Seven-point Polygon	Octagon

For smaller-sized designs, trace the above archetypal templates.

Enlarging base archetypal shapes

To enlarge the above archetypal templates first trace the selected shape. Rule lines from the centre point to each outer point of your shape extending each line as far as you wish to go (in this example we are enlarging our base shape by 20mm). Measure 20mm from each outer point creating an extended size. Join these points to create the new shape. Completing the base by using a compass to draw a circle, encasing the shape. Use this method when creating all archetypal shapes.

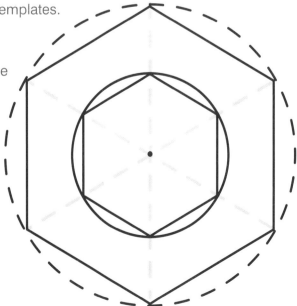

Above is an example of an archetypal shape used as an underlying template. By measuring equal distances from the centre the smaller base shape can be enlarged. Central guidelines can either run through the main corner points (A) or be drawn halfway between the dissecting lines (B).

Here are a further two examples where shapes from the previous page can be redrawn, building a more elaborate base.

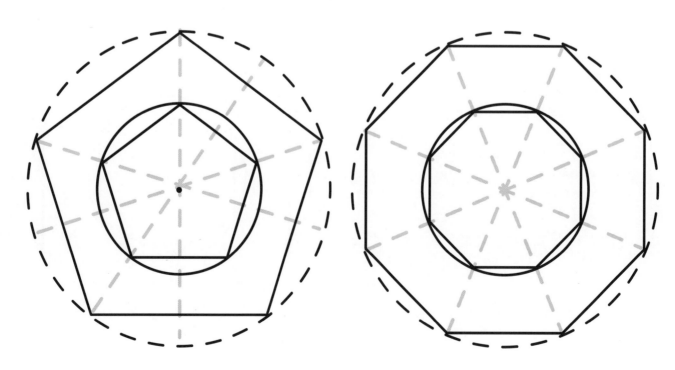

Exercise 2: Creation Emerging

This exercise highlights creation emerging through expansion and self-replication. Simple elliptical shapes that progress outward, creating symbolism of the butterfly, representing creation emerging into form. The chosen shapes are for fertility and harmony and promote a gently balanced expression of energy.

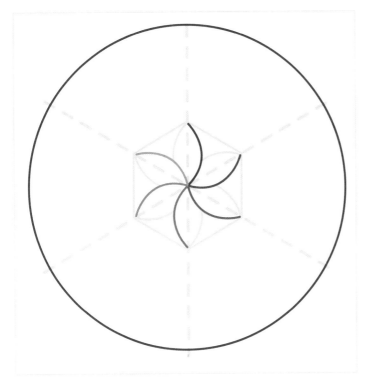

Step 1: Draw a 180mm square. Dissect it horizontally and vertically to find the centre point and draw a circle approximately 60% of the square, leaving space to add the outer petals. Trace the hexagon (from page 13) in the centre with a width of 36mm from side to side, not corner to corner. Join the opposite corners with a straight line through the centre extended out to the edge of the circle as shown.

Step 2: Draw a curved line on the right side of the upper vertical line connecting the top corner of the hexagon with the centre. Repeat this with the remaining five corners as indicated. Draw symmetrical three-quarter length lines on the left side of each guideline creating an overlapping effect.

Step 3: To draw butterflies start by measuring 32mm from the centre along each main guideline to mark point A (the horizontal midline of the butterfly) and 44mm to mark point A1 (the horizontal topline of the butterfly). Next measure halfway along each side of the hexagon to add six midlines for the vertical centre of each butterfly (B). On the top line measure 10mm either side of the B midline for the wingtips (C). Therefore the total height and width of the butterfly is 20mm (C to D).

Step 4: Draw the ellipse around the centre point (B) 10mm long (half on either side). Extend the curved line of the ellipse to join C and D. Then the two smaller curved lines between C and D to complete one half of the butterfly. Reverse this for the other side. Repeat this process for all five other butterflies, carefully erasing the hexagonal template when all butterflies are featured.

Step 5: To draw the teardrop shaped petals round the outer edge extend the main hexagonal guidelines (A) and midlines (B) from the edge of the circle a further 25mm. Measure halfway between A and B to mark line E. Starting at the tip of petal A draw a curved line to where the E line crosses the circle. Then draw a similar curved line from E up to B. Repeating this for the remaining eleven petals.

Step 6: The final step is for the curved lines to join the top left-hand wings (C) to the outer petal, point (F) This curved line should cross the line A at approximately 40mm from the centre. Then gently erase all guidelines and colour your completed design. Refer to the finished image within the colour section at the back of the book.

This final image has been coloured in violet and magenta tones, representing the harmonising energies of nature associated with inspiration and vitality. The butterflies reveal transformation and new life emerging. This is one example where animal symbols, geometric shapes and colours are combined to create a dynamic yet harmonious effect.

Symmetry and Shape

Basic geometric shapes are characteristic of all natural elements and can be shown to convey distinctive qualities within artwork. This image shows the evolving relationship between static and dynamic shapes at an elementary level. Active dynamic triangular shapes are used in the centre with red and magenta representing desire and activity. The more passive static shapes are used toward outer levels with blue tones for consolidation, structure and purpose. The points of balance are the hexagonal and oval shapes and the colour violet.

The Dynamics of Shape

Shapes can be divided into static, balancing and dynamic, respectively referring to passive, neutral and active qualities. Understanding the meaning of shapes together with their associated colours helps create symbolically rich designs.

Passive Static Shapes

The **circle.** Fullness and symmetrical balance. It can be either a full cycle of activity (completeness) or no activity (potential). It relates to the passive colour tones of white and light blue, and to quietly gentle animals associated with the moon, such as the whale, dolphin, otter and deer.

The **oval.** On its side depicts passivity. Its form can be seen naturally in pools and ponds, and in ripples of water. Relating to blue colourings and watery animals such as the dolphin, whale and swan.

The **octagon.** A static shape associated with structure. Blue and purple tones are used for qualities of universality and equalisation. Indicative of animals associated with the octagon shape are the turtle, lizard, spider, owl and octopus.

The **square.** A static shape representing inertia and solidity. When its points run vertically, as in the diamond, it becomes more expansive and dynamic and relates more to the colour yellow. Animals related to the square are the snake, turtle, butterfly and elephant.

Neutral Balancing Shapes

The **teardrop.** Balance between passive, circular and dynamic triangular shapes. It represents the formless taking form and the highest principles of life, such as purity, grace and refinement. Animals related to the teardrop are the dove, swan and phoenix.

The **oval.** In its vertical position symbolises the balance between formless and form and between static and active shapes. It works well with gold and purple tones, and the gently active energies of the swan and snake.

The **semicircle**. Considered to be a neutral shape depicting half full. It relates to the cool green and aqua-blue, the mid-point of the colour spectrum and the principle of communion. Animals related to the semicircle are the dove, dolphin and deer.

The **hexagon.** One of the most balancing of all shapes. Associated with the air element it characterises qualities of sustenance and balance while relating to green and grey colour tones. When coloured violet it is harmonising. Its representation works well in images containing dolphins, whales, swans and most birds.

Active Dynamic Shapes

The **ellipse.** Fertility, new growth and the passage from which life is born. It is a dynamic shape and natural colours are lime green and yellow. Resembling the eye in shape it may also be used to represent vision. Animals related to the ellipse are the bee, swallow and lizard.

The **diamond.** A dynamic shape associated with the productive processes. Expressing expansion qualities it relates well to yellow and orange, and being a powerful image it relates to the jaguar, tiger and lion.

The **pentagon.** A dynamic feminine shape associated with Mother Nature and the five elements of creation. Encompassing the principles of fertility and intercommunion with the colour green being prominent and associated animals are the dragon and parrot.

The **triangle.** Associated with activity, initiation and energy. Representing the transformation of life it relates to the fire elements of bright red and magenta. Its animals are fiery, such as the ram and phoenix, it can also symbolise new beginnings and inspiration, with the butterfly, and associated with the power of the horse.

Exercise 3: Desire Manifesting

In this exercise we combine animal totems and symbolism to create a gentle balance. Colours such as violet and magenta are used for refined attributes of desire associated with creativity, with both triangular shapes and the phoenix associated with empowerment and completion.

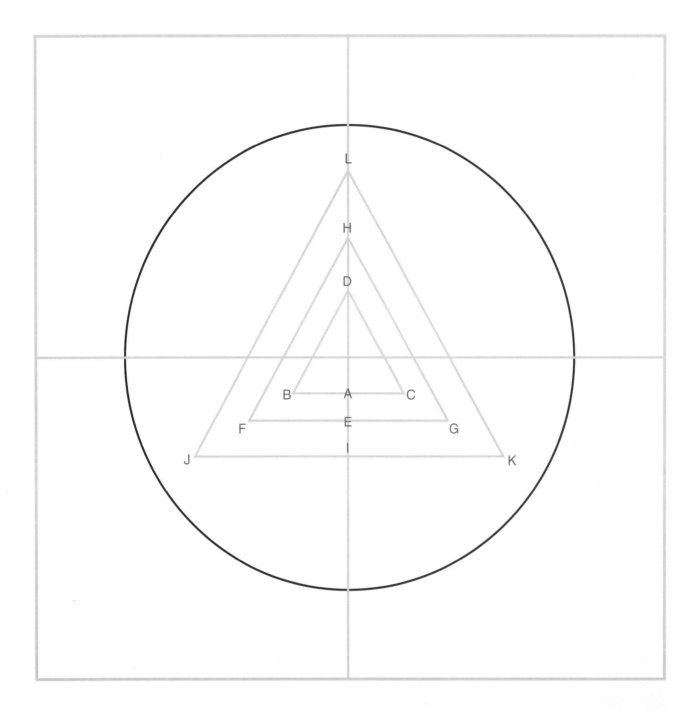

Step 1: Draw a 180mm square and dissect it horizontally and vertically to find the centre point. Next draw three faint triangles to be used as guidelines. Mark three points on the lower vertical axis — A (10mm), E (17mm) and I (26mm) — to position the triangle baselines. Then mark three points along the upper vertical axis — D (18mm), H (32mm) and L (49mm) — to mark the tips of the triangles. Using A, E and I as guides draw three horizontal baselines the following widths: B to C (32mm), F to G (55mm) and J to K (85mm). Then connect each baseline with the tip of each triangle. Finally using a compass, draw a surrounding circle with a diameter of 122mm.

Step 2: Starting with the two curved pathway lines draw below the birds, two curves starting from the tip of the small triangle through the bottom corners of the larger triangle finishing at the circle. Connect the tips of the two larger triangles with a small circle, representing the sun. (If you use a compass place halfway between points 2 and 3 to draw the circle.) Finally the phoenix and starfish symbols. As this is a freehand exercise either copy or trace the images using the above template as a guide for positioning. Finally, carefully erase the three triangles before adding the outer petals.

Observations

Both the geometric and freehand shapes have dynamic and fiery qualities. Keep the shapes symmetrically balanced on both sides of the image, persevering with any shapes or images which are unfamiliar or difficult. As the purpose of this exercise is to familiarise yourself with different shapes and forms you can practise separately, then copy or trace your final image either side.

Step 3: Draw the six petal shapes around the circle. Begin by tracing the six cornerpoints of the hexagon on page 13, (represented by the six rings) aligning the centre of the hexagon with the centre of your image. (unnecessary to draw the whole hexagon as this will interfere with your design.) Rule in six faint guidelines from the centre through each point 35mm past the edge of the circle, forming the centre line for each petal (A). Measure halfway along the lines to mark the points for each petal (B). Following the same process for exercise 2 draw half the petal on one side of the A line, repeating this for the other. (connect tip A to the circle at line B). Repeat this for all petals. Draw in the smaller curved lines inside each petal as shown and erase all guidelines.

Step 4: The final step will add in the palm trees and additional lines surrounding the sun and birds, also left in outline form opposite for colouring. The colours below are appropriate for this image.

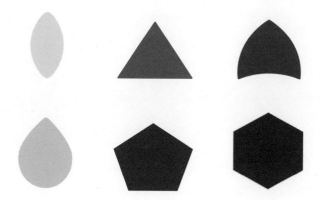

Creative Colouring

The following pages allow the opportunity to colour some pre-drawn mandalas. Each can also be traced or enlarged. Refer to the colour section at the back of the book for inspiration and feel free to experiment with different colours and shadings. The phoenix in this image represents transformation and relates well to red, magenta and violet tones. Gold and orange provide a complimentary balance where needed.

Throughout many cultures the peacock is a symbol for the glory and majesty of material creation, perfection and sustenance. The central lotus, new life emerging while the rising sun suggests power and vitality of the new dawn and the awakening of life's energies. The water brings in the fuel which sustains and nurtures all life and indeed the process of birth and transformation. The eight outer petals complete the image, now revealing structure and balance.

This mandala depicts the lunar, or feminine, energies of creation. It is both dynamic and lively, although is better suited to passive colours. Related to the owl is white, with deep blues and purples signifying lunar energies of the moon and night sky. The garland of jasmine flowers is shown in white or pink, as are the roses. The lingam, or cosmic egg shape, being garlanded is symbolic of feminine energies within creation and positioned vertically symbolises the generating masculine force or seed source of creation.

Doves represent peace, hope, faith and virtues such as grace and purity. They are associated with both gently refined masculine energies and the feminine qualities of receptivity, mutuality and openness, and with the air and water elements. Colours are soft pastel blue tones as these depict gentle qualities, particularly peace. Light violet tones can be used effectively as they too support grace and refinement.

Exercise 4: The Art of Preservation

This exercise combines animal totems, symbolism and basic geometry, highlighting the principle of preservation and balance.

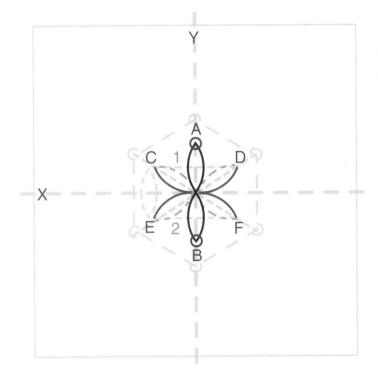

(These images not to scale.)

Step 1: Draw a square 180mm x 180mm and dissect it horizontally and vertically to find the centre point. Faintly trace the hexagon template from page 13 in the centre to act as a guide. Mark the two diagonal guidelines through the centre of the hexagon connecting opposite corners.

Step 2: Measure out from the centre 12mm along each guideline to mark the points A through F. Draw in the six ellipse shapes each approximately 5mm wide. If using a compass place the anchor at each point (starting with A and B), open it the length of one ellipse shape and draw in the curved line from C to D, then E to F. Repeat this for each corner.

Step 3: Draw the six oval shapes, measure 150% of the length of the ellipse shape (18mm) along each of the six guidelines and mark the tip (H). Measure half way between points A and C to obtain the middle point (I) where the two ovals will intersect. Draw a freehand curve from point H crossing over the point I, finishing at point J. Repeat this process on the other side to form the top half of the oval shape. Repeat this for the other five ellipses.

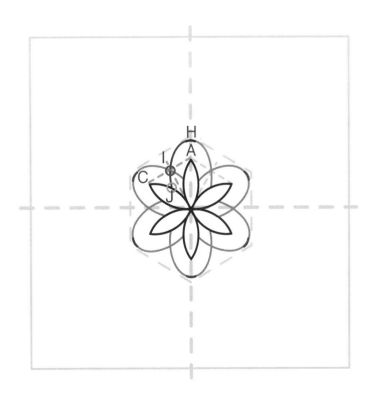

Step 4: The six-point star shape and six ank symbols. First draw the two circles, the inner 122mm across and the outer 132mm. Extend the twelve central guidelines past the outer circle approximately 30mm (adding the petals later). Next join the points K, L and M at the edge of the inside circle to form the first triangle. Draw a second triangle slightly smaller with a gap of 5mm. Repeat this process for the second triangle joined at points N, O and P. Erasing lines where the two triangles cross, indicating an interwoven pattern.

Step 5: Draw in the ank symbols associated with eternal life. Using the guidelines at the intersection of the triangle points. (produce these in freehand). Alternatively you may practice on a separate sheet of paper and trace six times for a more symmetrical image.

Step 6: Draw the six outer petals following the method from the previous exercise. Starting at the centreline tip (Q) draw a curved line to the edge of the circle (P) again for the opposite side of the line. Repeat this process five times to produce completed petals. Then the smaller inner curved lines 4mm apart to align with the curved stem of the ank as shown.

Step 7: Finally the dolphins within the six outer petals. This is a freehand exercise. So style each side of the dolphin ensuring it appears symmetrical. Again, you might like to practice on a separate sheet of paper. Then all dolphin outlines except those that cross under the 5mm section of the circle and star. Erase all guidelines when finished.

This completed mandala has been left in outline form for colouring. The central triangular hexagon is for preservation of life energies. Choose colours green and aqua blue. Addressing balance in the polarities of nature, such as creation and destruction, light and dark, etc. For peace, harmony and purity the dolphins are coloured with blue, violet and white. For the ank symbol, deep blue and indigo associated with eternal life, green relating to growth and fertility, while violet and gold represent transcendence as the ank denotes immortality. The other shapes can vary in colour, and with the section at the back of the book more understanding may be gained in recognising appropriate shapes and forms for the most harmonising effect.

Symbols From The Natural World

Symbolism throughout the world of nature is vast and various. In designing mandalas we create our own 'ideal world' and can include any combination of animals, symbols or shapes to express our vision. Both animal and natural symbols have a deeper meaning beyond their physical form, reflecting their true essence and beauty. Animals live instinctively and therefore associate more naturally, living in harmony with all. The symbols on this page have been included within the following pages.

The moon is of course very symbolic representing the feminine qualities of creation. As a water element, it emphasises principles of mutability and receptivity and it is considered a gentle influence. It can be placed in the mandala to convey the fullness of creation.

The lotus, the life force; opening to the light of life. It represents birth from the water element, reflecting emergence from the fluid environment of the womb. Life being born from fire (sun) and water elements relates to magenta (masculine) or blue and white (feminine).

The conch shell is known for the cosmic sound of creation and is found throughout many cultural traditions. It relates to the call of a new day and an ancient remembrance of life emerging from the water element. It symbolises the awakening of knowledge and is said to dispel ignorance and illusion.

The butterfly signifies transformation of the life force from one stage to the next. A central image in the mandala, It reveals how the power of creation is transmuted. Representing freedom and new beginnings in the journey of life, its preferred colours are yellow and violet.

The starfish indicates the five-fold principle of creation represented by the five senses and five elements earth, air, fire, water and ether (or space). Generally it is associated with the earth element as the five elements combined create physical forms. It has a natural connection to the water element and can be used to enhance the cosmic feminine energies, often symbolised by a five-pointed star.

The dolphin is an adventurous animal moving in tune with the rhythms and breath of life. It is associated with water energies, communication, free flowing expression of emotions and the colours blue and aqua, while suited to violet tones associated with harmony and inspiration. In the mandala opposite the dolphins symbolise the call of the new dawn and attunement to the light.

The water element is represented by a passive half-full/half-empty bowl denoting balance. The water element may also be depicted by rippling effects as shown in some of the following mandalas. Water represents the continual movement of life in a peaceful and balanced way and relates well to blue tones, particularly aqua blue.

Creative Colouring

The following mandalas, may be traced or enlarged prior to colouring. Refer to the colour section at the back and feel free to experiment with various colours and shadings.

This mandala centring around the peaceful, playful energies of nature are most evident in the early hours of the morning. The rising sun represents the light and inspiration of a new day as does the conch shell with its sound of creation. The butterfly represents new beginnings, harmony and the spirit of freedom. The lotus, symbolises emergence of all that is new, pure and good in life. The starfish depicts the five elements of nature and the dolphins, freedom, playfulness and the breath of life.

Emerging energies of nature. The morning sun is for the light and inspiration of a new day, as does the central butterfly indicating new beginnings, harmony and the spirit of freedom. The unicorn is a mythical creature embracing intuition and vision and here represents grace, harmony and insight. In this image the snake is latent potential energy representing the hidden or unknown.

This image depicts group spirit and the harmonious intercommunion of nature. Wolves in particular symbolise group loyalty and the relationship with their surroundings. These communal creatures are associated with simplicity, faithfulness and loyalty with a reverence and closeness to nature. Representing earth, air and water energies, colouring should predominantly be blue and green tones.

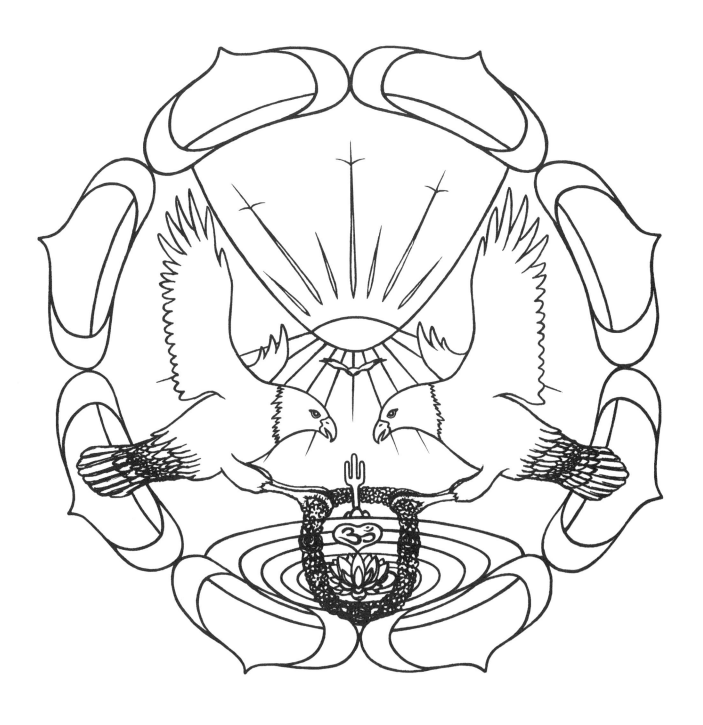

Awakening energies of nature. The sun shows the dawning light of a new day and evokes new beginnings. The eagle stands for the spirit of freedom, highest virtues and principles. In this particular image the lotus is latent potential energy, emerging and blossoming of life energies, promoting all that is new, pure and good in life.

Exercise 5: Drawing Whales

These features are designed to develop freehand drawing skills using as inspiration various forms of sea creatures. Their environment, the ocean, embraces the submerged potential of creation in the same way human life starts in the fluid environment of the womb. Water relates to emotional and creative expression, and the ocean is home to many creatures which may be included with spontaneity.

Step 1: First draw the faint outline of the oval shapes and curved lines as shown. These provide a basic framework.

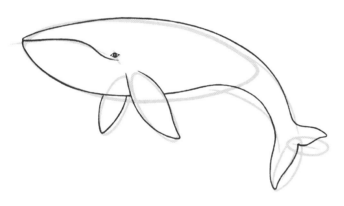

Step 2: Next darken the outline as shown. The main point to emphasise where the various shapes meet. Curves and points are important, giving the whale its unique characteristics.

Step 3: Finally, shown the more detailed lines such as under the mouth, gills etc. The shadow marks generally appear on the underside. Lines may also be pencilled, highlighting and edging contours, such as at the end of the fins.

Observations
For these exercises work from light to dark. Start by using faint pencil lines for outlines and when confident with the image use darker lines, adding final definition and detail.

Exercise 6: Drawing Seahorses

Step 1: Firstly draw the faint outline shapes for the seahorses. Adding smaller oval shapes assists the flow of curves for the symmetry of the seahorse.

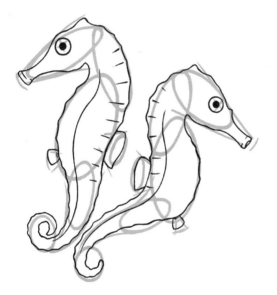

Step 2: Next define the outline using the initial lighter lines as guides. The seahorse has rippled contours along its back, illustrated by using smaller curves.

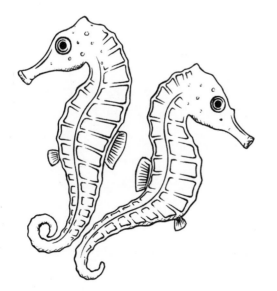

Step 3: Finally, complete the detailed features such as the body segments and fin lines. Maintaining balance between pointed tips and smooth corners is important when drawing body segments. Random styling of segments will give a more natural effect.

Exercise 7: Drawing Angelfish

Step 1: Firstly draw the faint outline of the oval shapes and curved lines. The angelfish is almost entirely composed of oval shapes with simple curves for the fin and body lines.

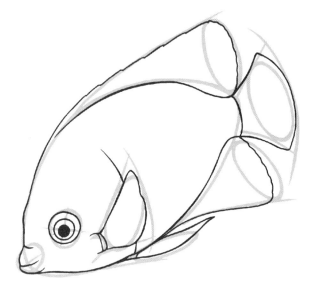

Step 2: Next emphasise the specific features. The angelfish generally has soft curves in its bodyline with a few points at the edges of its fins.

Step 3: Finally, include the more detailed lines of scales and fins, adding extra lines to highlight patterns, edging and shadows. The shadows of course appear on the underside.

Exercise 8: Drawing an Octopus

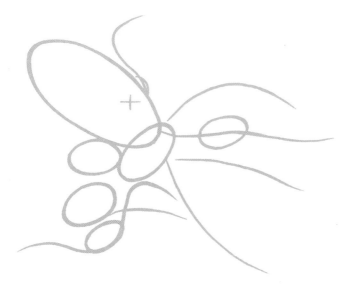

Step 1: Firstly, the faint outline of the oval shapes for the body and additional curved lines for the tentacles.

Step 2: Next draw the basic outline for the body and tentacles. The octopus has a balloon shaped body and tentacles like a rubber band or lasso. Randomly placed tentacles make its appearance more natural.

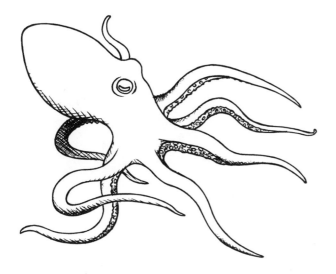

Step 3: Finally, colour the more detailed lines on the underbody of the octopus adding shadow marks to the underside. Lines may also be pencilled to highlight edging contours, such as the suction cups which the octopus uses to cling to surfaces.

Exercise 9: A Creation Concept

Using free-flowing forms as inspiration, this exercise depicts a scenic image symbolising birth, growth and fertility. The whale totem in particular is associated with birth and conceptual beginnings representing energies surfacing into form. This exercise develops skills in both curved and symmetrical lines as well as illustrating how particular shapes may reflect strong imagery. It also incorporates stereographic style (mirrored from left to right) adding harmony and balance to the overall design.

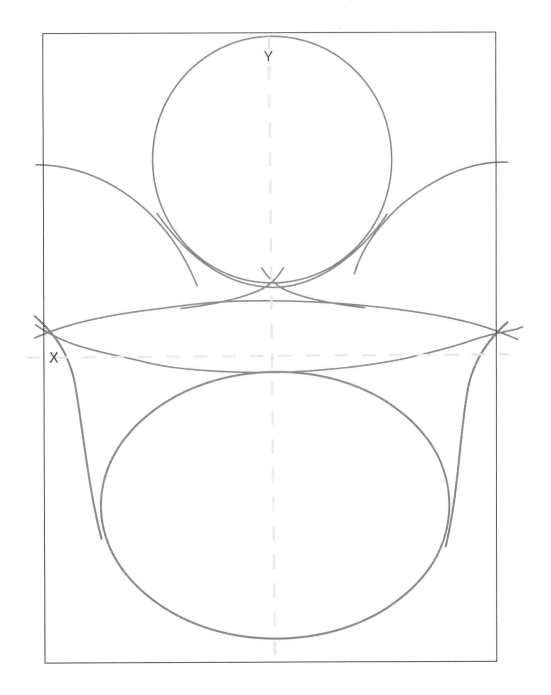

Step 1: Using an A4 sheet of paper draw a rectangle 190mm x 255mm. Dissect this vertically and horizontally with faint guidelines finding the centre point. (The X and Y axis lines are not crucial, however they keep a symmetrical balance from left to right and top to bottom.) Using this image as a guide for proportions and measurements lightly draw both curved shapes and lines. These will act as the foundation from which to draw a natural scene, including forms showing hills, beach, sun and trees.

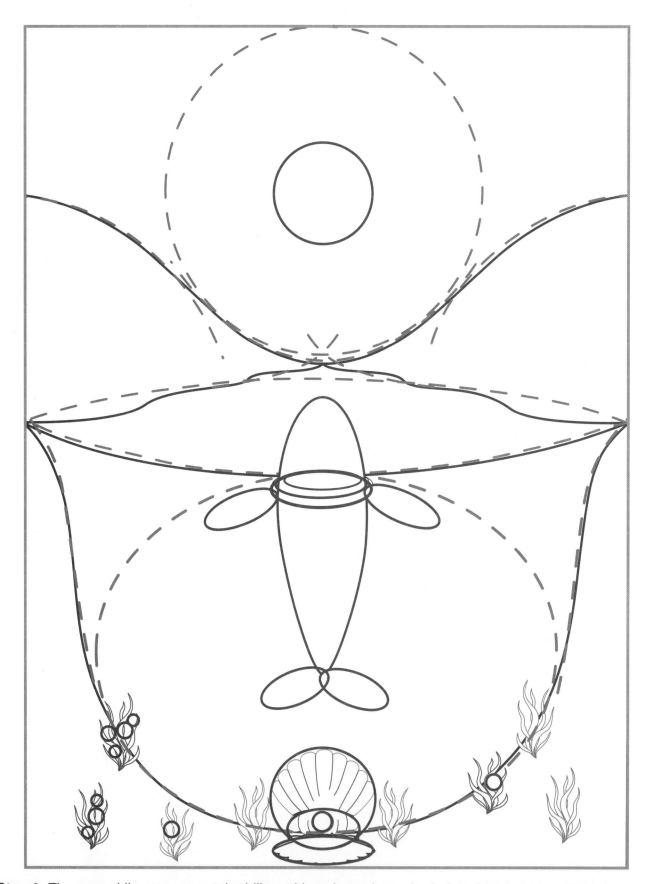

Step 2: The curved lines represent the hills and beach as shown in dark indigo (use the dashed lines as guides). Next the circular and oval shapes (violet) for the whale, moon, scallop shell and so on. For preferred positioning refer to the finished version, however, at this stage general placement is acceptable. With the sea grass use the smaller circles to assist with the flow.

Step 3: Add more detailed darker lines for the whale, moon and sea shell. These forms are reasonably simple by using curved and elliptical shapes. The seagrass on the ocean bed is shown with flowing curves to indicate movement. The palm trees require simple guidelines when positioning their rows. Finally, the starfish on the following page creates a natural effect. The following page has been left in outline form for colouring.

Exercise 10: Duplication and Expansion

Here we show pentagonal geometry showing the five senses and five elements, earth, air, fire, water and ether. Duplication and expansion are combined with basic geometry and animal totems, creating an omni-directional mandala, expanding to all directions.

Step 1: Draw a square 180mm x 180mm and dissect it horizontally and vertically, finding the centre point. Faintly trace the pentagon template from page 13 (aligning both centres exactly) making it approximately 28mm in diameter (final image on page 55). Rule faint guidelines from the centre through each corner point and again through the midpoint of each side of the pentagon.

Step 2: Create the smaller central pentagonal flower by drawing five small ellipses on the five main corner guidelines approximately half the distance from the edge to the centre (7mm long). Repeat this shape slightly larger on the other five guidelines in between (12mm) and a third time (10mm) to form the outer circle of half ellipse shapes as shown.

Step 3: Extend the five main guidelines 50mm to mark the tip of the turtle head (A). Extend the other five guidelines 43mm to mark where the front flippers meet (B). On this line also mark at 23mm (C) and 17mm (D) where the lower flippers meet.

Step 4: Draw the first turtle outline halfway on either side of the top vertical line. Start with the turtle head at point A continuing to the flipper tip at point B, then to the lower flipper through C and D finishing at the tail. Repeat this for the other side. Maintaining the same process for the remaining four turtle shapes. (For a cleaner finish practise on a separate sheet of paper and then trace five times.)

Step 5: Using a compass draw two circles around the turtles approximately 110mm and 122mm in diameter. Adding the outer lotus petals by using the 'draw half and reflect' method used earlier. Use the ten guidelines from the central pentagon shape as midlines for the tips and bases of the petals.

Step 6: The final step. To add five elliptical pentagonal shapes along the five midlines in between the turtle flippers. Measure approximately 31mm along each line to mark the centre of each shape (E) and again 25mm to mark the length of one ellipse (F). Using the central pentagonal shape as a guide, create the five ellipse shapes for each flower.

Observations

The duplication and expansion of the central pentagonal ellipses reflect the principle of self-replication. The turtles similarly mirror the expansion of the pentagonal effect. In this design there are seven pentagons formed by joining tips or outer points.

This final image is coloured harmoniously in violets and blues. Using shading will enhance the effect of energy radiating from the centre (light colours in general have an expansive illuminating effect while darker colours are more grounding and consolidating.) Symbolic colours have been used to reflect the unique qualities of the shapes and images. Simple dot and star patterns are featured around the outer ring to give a more stylised effect, complementing the existing geometry.

Exercise 11: Harmony Within Form

Here we will use the 'Flower of Life' pattern (shown below) as a template which provides symmetrically balanced foundation. Many forms incorporating curved and straight lines can be created by gazing at this matrix. For this though swans have been chosen as central images embracing grace, perfection and harmony. Further curved lines and shapes compliment this template. The emphasis on elliptical and heart shapes convey principles of emergence, fertility and growth, providing a balance between both passive and dynamic energies.

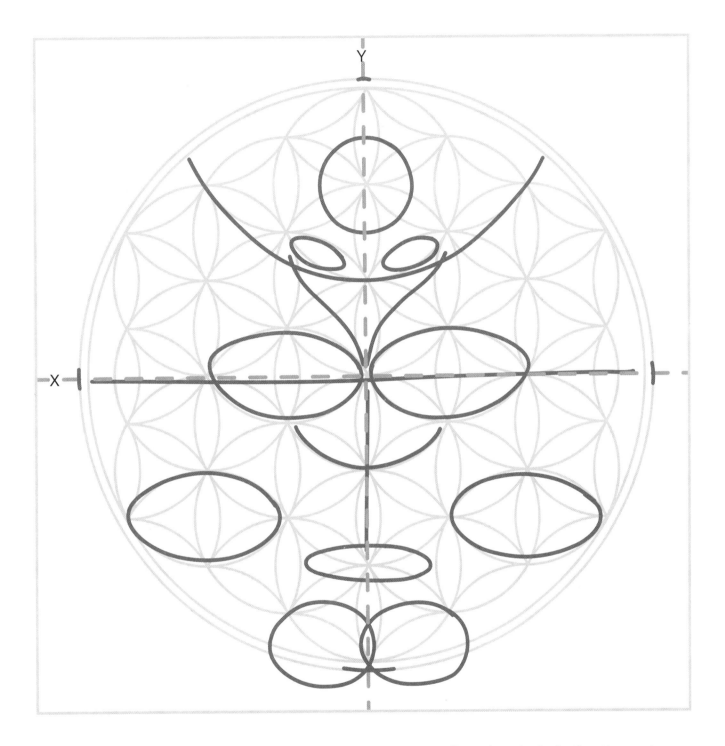

Step 1: Draw a square 180mm x 180mm and dissect it horizontally and vertically finding the centre point. Then placing your drawing sheet over the 'Flower of Life' template on page 61 and mark the edges (top, bottom, left and right) as shown above. Next the rough oval shapes for primary images, adding the remaining structural lines as shown.

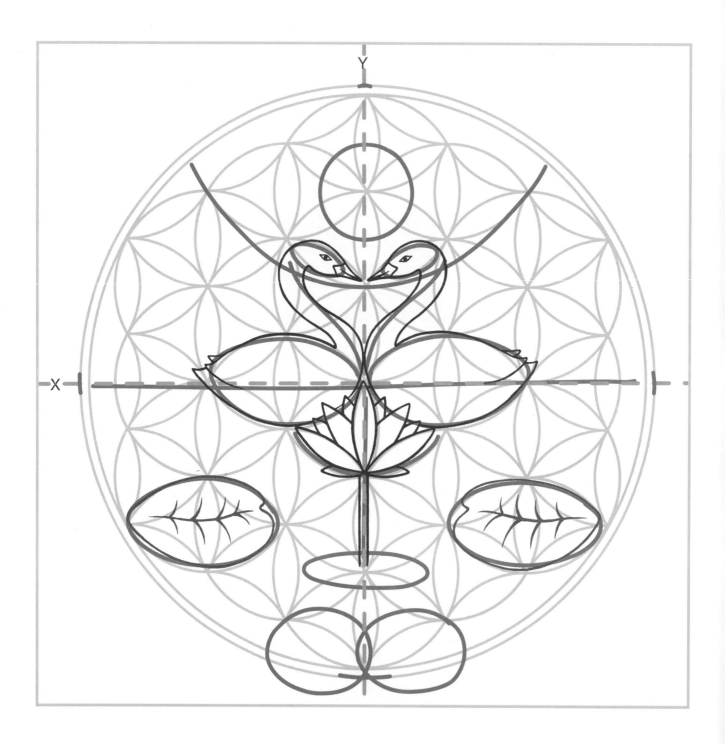

Step 2: Using the final image as a reference include the lotus flower and swans using the underlying outlines as a guide. While exact symmetry is sometimes maintained, it is not essential. Using a similar process for harmony, add the sun and lotus leaves. With a faint outer circle, helping to maintain overall symmetry.

Step 3: Darken to clearly define the central image, adding the remaining water lines to enhance the feeling of movement. As with most curved lines and shapes there is no fixed method. Practising freehand will help with a sense of proportions and appreciating when it 'feels' right. The central horizontal waterline is a randomly curving line, breaking the mirror image effect whilst making it more spontaneous but gentle.

This final version of this swan mandala has been left blank for colouring. The swans represent harmony and grace and relate well to violet and white. The lotus is for new life and in this peaceful setting works well with blue and white. The water element represents the continual movement of life in a peaceful and balanced way, relating to aqua blues and greens; the mirrored effect once again adds balance and harmony. The circle within the top represents fullness and completeness, depicted as either the sun (using vitalising warmer colours such as red, orange or yellow tones) or the moon with cooler white or blue tones.

Flower of Life Geometric Matrix

Colour Qualities

This section explains the symbolic qualities associated with individual colours. Using and combining colours in thoughtful ways undoubtedly enhances the artwork.

White

White symbolises purity and liberation promoting energy and the highest potential. In Tantric art it represents the masculine aspect of a deity. It associates with water and often assigned to feminine planets such as the Moon and Venus, purifying and pacifying the emotions. White is often used to provide contrast and bridge other colours.

Violet

Violet is associated with harmony and when becoming more inert and as deep purple, in action it returns to its original source. In its mid tones it conveys neutrality and its brighter shades, higher transformation. In its light shades violet associates with tranquility and as darker purple, more deeply passive. This is a unique combination of the coming together of two opposite energies.

Magenta

In mandalas it is used to evoke the goddess. It is the passion and vitality of the creative force merged with the white and violet rays and signifies aspiration. Magenta is commonly used to colour triangles and the Sun.

Pink

Pink has a calming and harmonising effect of the emotions and promotes deeper creative urges. Pink can symbolise creativity manifesting and the potential for refined sensitivity. In mandalas pink is usually for gentle feminine energies and used for colouring auspicious goddesses, the Sun, the Moon, Mars and Venus merged in unison representing male and female balance.

Red

Red associates with desire, fertility and manifestation. In Tantric art it is used to represent the fire element and the feminine attributes of a deity. In association with astrological influences however, red relates to the masculine planets of Mars and the Sun (as fire red and magenta) are appropriate colour for triangles.

Orange

Orange is used to show the gentle masculine or feminine energies of the rising sun, the full moon (as pastel) and the energies of auspicious goddesses. Blended with golden yellows and pinks represents a gentle creative force. Pastel orange represents maternal and nurturing energies and is considered the more feminine or purer expression of the above.

Yellow

Yellow represents expansive qualities and is often used to colour the outer square or perimeter of a mandala. Also signifying the earth element. In its saffron tone it represents joy, abundance, general wealth and good fortune.

Gold

Golden tones in the tawny green-brown range are traditionally used to show negative and destructive energies of wrathful forces. Relating to murky colours, such as a swamp it promotes turbulent chaotic energies. Pure gold (metallic) in striking contrast depicts the highest of vibrations. Relating to perfection and transcendence it is used to emphasise shapes representing the highest virtues.

Lime

Lime is used for fertile and active life-giving energies, observing new growth and the vitality of spring. Lime can be used in the outer square for active and communicative life energies and has invigorating qualities. Lime has a vitalising and stimulating effect and generally only needs to be used in small amounts in artwork as it can be overpowering.

Green

Green, linked to lime, also fosters communication and exchange and reflects similar properties, such as growth and fertility. As mid-green it depicts interconnection and as a cooler emerald and blue-green shade implies calmness. Green is often used to signify the air element and the balancing aspect of nature as it can be either warm (active) or cool (passive).

Aqua

Although not traditionally used in the mandala this colour is effective when working with higher expression and harmony within the emotions. It fosters artistic freedom of expression and refined sensitivity. This colour suits the elements air and water.

Blue

Blue in its lighter tones is similar to aqua and can be found in some mandalas and yantras to represent gentle passive deities. It is symbolically used for the air element in light pastel blues promoting openness and expansiveness. Blue relates to gentle and refined expression and the energies coloured by the throat chakra.

Deep Blue

As the blue ray approaches its mid tones it starts relating to neutrality and passiveness. In traditional sacred art, blue is often used to reveal the qualities of structure and contraction (dark blue). Deep blue also relates to withdrawal, or receding and connecting with the life source vibration.

Indigo

Indigo represents integration, purposefulness and structural integrity and is utilised when defining boundaries. The most invigorating of the blue tones it promotes insight, relating to the light of life. In its deeper tones it encourages insight into more contemplative mysteries.

Black

Black defines the light and all other colours. It is used in mandalas for border designs and boundaries, representing structure. Through qualities of negativity and devolution it is also associated with the earth element. Black can be used to depict negative or wrathful energies, or inertia and darkness in general.

Grey

In its smoky colour grey is traditionally used in mandalas to depict the element ether. In its light smoky tones it is associated with air and to the unseen and invisible energies. Used in the mandala it emphasises both beauty and perfection.

Animal Symbols

The deer symbolises innocence, gentleness and purity and is associated with the energies of the moon and its feminine attunement in life's natural rhythms. The deer reaches out in gentleness to touch the wounded hearts and minds of those lost or confused. Colouring ideally in white.

The horse is a symbol of power and vitality. When associated with the sun, its appropriate colours are magenta and red. It embodies femininity and at that stage relates to white. When relating to the refinement of desire, and sensuality, suggested colours are light violet.

The tiger symbolises, passion and refined sensuality. Tigers display great motherly devotion and in the Indian tradition are the vehicle of many goddesses as they show courage of the heart and the balancing of power. It is strongly tied with the colour orange.

The lion expresses the coming into one's own power. It is dignified, royal and strong, playing out a balance between the sun and moon. Lions symbolise courage and the expression of a non-domineering power, relating well to orange and yellow.

The coyote signifies balance between wisdom and playfulness and is useful in awakening the magic and mystery of childlike characteristics. A trickster that loves fun, the coyote brings about simplicity and trust fostering a new visionary perspective. A re-awakening of humour and intellect in balanced proportions. It relates well to the colour yellow.

The dragon is an ancient totem representing energetic potential. Shown in many colours the it effectively combines both growth and fertility associated with green. In yellow it depicts expansion illumination and abundance, also effective with light blue and aqua tones.

The lizard represents intuitivity and subtle perception symbolising the balance between the waking and dreaming states. It can provide a profound connection to the Dreamtime and is a valuable totem helping to bridge the conscious and subconscious mind, bringing foresight and vision.

The dolphin conveys the power of breath and sound communication and emotions in balance. Between air and water representing innocence and freedom. The dolphin is calming and tuned into the universal flow of life. Indigo, mid- blue and aqua tones are appropriate colours.

Symbolises immortality and sometimes the unknown, the snake relates well to the colour green for fertility and magenta for transmutation. Equally the source of hidden potential is captured with deep blue and black colours.

Templates

On the following pages basic templates are shown which allow the artist to create more extensive and of course personalised art work. The centre in many cases is left blank for you to draw your own design. You can use the symbols and techniques learnt throughout this book, or design your own in a free-style manner.

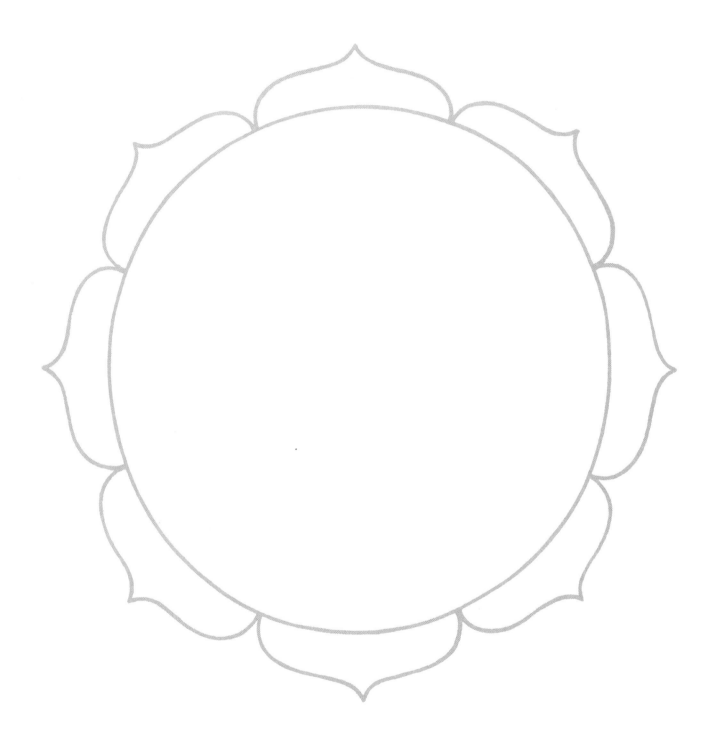

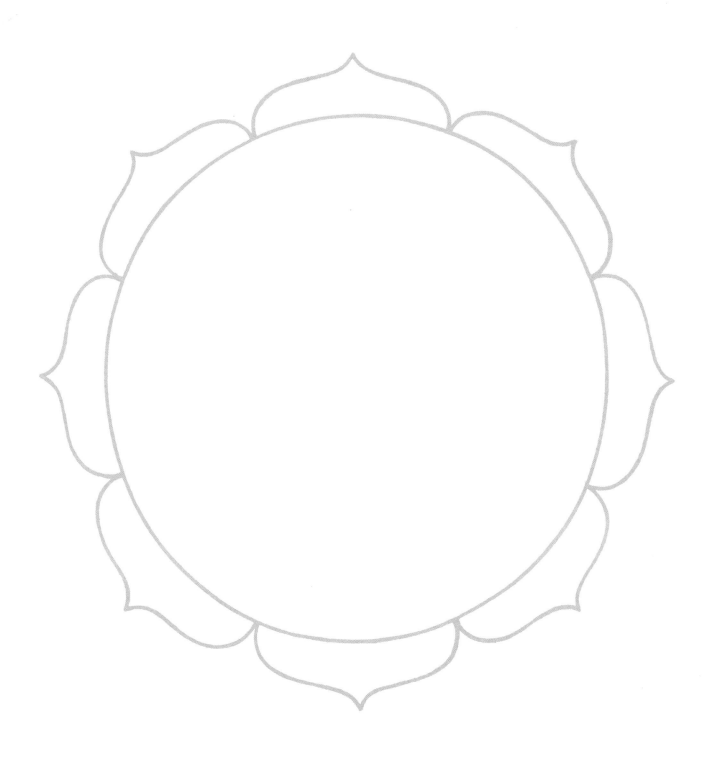